I0141785

Coffee House Memories

Poems by
Brian J. Noggle

Jeracor Group LLC
5643 South Haseltine Road, Brookline MO 65619

ISBN-13: 978-0-9832123-4-8

Table of Contents

Preface

To write a self-indulgent preface or not to write a self-indulgent introduction? Strangely, this has proven to be the most difficult part of compiling this volume. I have decided to hedge: Instead of several pages waxing prosaically lyrical about the coffee houses in which I spent the first half of my twenties, I'll just briefly mention that I wrote most of these poems on yellow pad in a beat-up leather binder at the Grind, or MoKaBe's, or the Oasis, or the Brew Bayou, or other coffee shops.

I've also included two chapbooks that I offered in those years in their original order: *Unrequited* from 1994 and *Deep Blue Shadows* from 1995. The following poems in this volume have already appeared in various periodicals: "A brash young man, ideas set…." first appeared in the 1991 *Marquette Journal Literary Edition;* "Chance Encounter", "Homecoming '93: A Collage", "Upon A Snowy Pillow…", "Falling Snow", and "Third Floor Eyes" appeared in the Spring 1994 *Marquette Journal*; "Somebody Else's Problem" appeared in Volume 2, Issue 1 (Summer 1994) of *The Scream*; "But Through The Fifth Floor Hospital Panes…" appeared in the 1996 issue of *Prolog*; "A Dark Café, Monday, 8:50pm" appeared in Volume 3, Issue 3 (Winter 1996) *Sink Full of Dishes*; and "Deb of the Dark" appeared as "Debutante of the Dark" in the Winter 1997 *Artisan Journal.*

Remembering Dog Days

As I slinked the bedroom's worn night path
The clouds burst and
I drank the shining moon,
Shimmered, and was elsewhere;
I splashed across the silver cool night,
Lolling tongue laughter with my pack.
We chased the neon scents of women
and dreams we half-only had.
I touched my paunch and pate, thick and thin,
Dispelling the vision; my howling days over.
Slipping beneath the comforting blankets,
I yawned and stretched amid my suburban pride,
Slept, and forgot the dog days all again.

The blue-silver early motel morning light…

The blue-silver early motel morning light
Trickled through the stolid curtain dam
To pool amid the moonsea blacks and greys
Across the barren desk, the tangled floor and bed.

Beneath the barbed-wool blankets you dream
Alone, I augur each breath, or sigh
To pluck unknown stars for meaning, for
What actors play across the stage within.
The cotton rustle in the chair, perhaps,
Transmutes to the slide of lovers' hands on skin.

Slow motion minutes and pendulous breaths
Whisper together, conspirators,
Until you slip the slumber's selfish grasp
And share your daylit dreams with me.

Red Is Just The Color Of Her Hair

Red as a wildfire sweeping
like a heavy summer breeze over the plain,
digesting the dragging grass and brush,
plowing furrows in the newly fertile soil
for daisies to spread their roots.

Red as a poppy swaying
in gentle gasps of wind
on a day of foolish dreams buzzing
flower to flower.

Red like a sunset tugging
the downy clouds to nestle against its chin
through the dream of night.

And red is just the color of her hair.

Lingering

Car window winds mingle sweet berry scents
Her hair, the air entices, was here, now there,
caressing heedless pillow cases.
Clinging morning stillness impresses
humid kisses on my neck and cheek, She
giggles behind the corners of consciousness
walks in the periphery of my dreams
whispers from the tall grass passing by.

Central Illinois Solo

Thundering south across the Illinois plane,
A herd of diesels growl to challenge foreign cars
And sedans plodding endlessly on
Thin strips of pavement stretched across the corn.
Inside a seventy mile-per-hour asylum,
I howl at the other drivers,
other beads on the strings of time,
dots on an unconnected line.
I wail the pilgrims on the radio,
shrieking their gods of pop love lie bleeding
along the highway side, caught in the rushing light
of youth and energy, and thrown aside with a thump
that rattles teeth and hands upon the wheel.
I rage, I shriek, I roar into the wind—

the quiet time is over....
No longer she sleeps, reclined and half turned,
   in the passenger seat,
breathing deep and lightly scented for the ride
No more will she blink slow, stretch like a Persian,
and cast lightening eyes across the crops and me
to ask, "Where are we?"
I could reply, certainly, softly, over the whisper of the radio,
"Six miles south of Tonica."
And she would smile, and try, but slip back to sleep.

No, that quiet time is over—
Despair, delusion, illusion, confusion swirl, four winds
Driving doubts like thunderheads across the prairie.
Recriminations and accusations echoed tantrum against the
   windshield.
Yet I sing with the storm
With strobing flashes of hindsight and thundering claps of
   I-don't-give-a-damn,
I hurtle into the darkness,
screaming sentiments too simple to repress,
as speeds too sane to be startling.

Exploring, we discovered Bee Tree park…

Exploring, we discovered Bee Tree Park.
Tree branches laced like lazy fingers behind our head,
above the trail, above the naked rock,
where neon graffiti was worn to earthen tones.
The slow Mississippi whispered by.
Fingers woven like dreams and the night
  before falling asleep.
Her warm palm pulsing, we paused
to watch the barges wander down
and sip the summer breeze.
Her voice murmured coolly in my ears,
she spilled her hair over my shoulder,
maple syrup dripping down my chest,
"This would be a great place to make love."
I smiled, ruffling kisses through her hairs,
a butterfly on a field of clover,
and rustled in her ear, "We are."

It's always more than sex to sleep with you…

It's always more than sex to sleep with you.
Don't get me wrong; I like to tangle sheets
and hungry scents and taste the salty dew
of glistening sweat where heavy brow meets
soft eyelids closed, relaxed. I'll kiss them, too,
and sample other slow seduction sweets.
But I run out of juice, won't thump my chest
and say I don't, and so I like the rest:
I like to lie, arms wrapped around you, deep
in comfortable darkness where the moon projects
odd patterns on the walls. I want to keep
you safe and warm as winter licks our necks.
You mumble love and slowly fall asleep;
these moments worth much more than simple sex.

Remember me in steaming showers where…

Remember me in steaming showers where
you loosen tensions from the day and think
that I massage your shoulders, white and bare,
my touch so warm it turns your skin to pink.
My fingers trickle through your clinging hair
and stinging shampoo kisses make you blink.
But if a shower too quickly runs to cold from hot,
let soft bath waters assure you I will not.
Imagine me there when you close your eyes
amid the bubbles of your bath, my hand
there in the subtle motions, stroking thighs,
smooth palms across your belly, lightly tanned,
and over scented neck up to the mouth that lies
above the water, crying your demand.

It would have been the perfect night…

It would have been the perfect night—
The first breath of autumn stirred the hairs on my arms;
the soft weight of a workday done
settled pleasantly on my shoulders
and blended my thoughts into pastel profundities.
A cool mist softened the night,
a night alive with potential
for warm drinks in cold hands,
quiet moments among tangled blankets.
The night blurred with impossibility,
your cool hand, the brief smile after a whispered word.
Beyond the west horizon,
where slick streets meet strip mall light,
you waste fading smiles on harriers, hurriers, and retail.
I pull greyness closer and shuffle east.
It would have been the perfect night

Once

Once I walked a young woman
to her dorm, the warm light spilling
into the crisp spring night;
we, wrapped in the gossamers of the future,
didn't care the cold.
Beyond the glassed-in comfort of a home,
we tickled each other's intellect
and sparked in each other's eyes.
"Perform your poetry!" I demanded,
perched upon a flagstone wall.
She did, and so did I, beneath the open April sky.
Possibility fluttered in the breeze,
snapping and crackling like a flame:
I left her that way that night,
back-lit softly by a lobby,
the Milwaukee wind gently teasing her hair.
As I go on, spinning life more tightly
from fibrous possibilities taken,
some tendrils remain unwoven.
These I leave, to twist in my fingertips,
and remind myself, once.

I've tossed off poems like handfuls of gravel...

I've tossed off poems like handfuls of gravel,
half-hearted, against unlit second story panes.
I've hurled dreams like sand into the wind,
each speck gritting my hair and stinging my eyes.
I've pitched my years like green twigs onto a flame,
smothering the fire with fuel too young.
I've cast off friends like lines from shore,
no more to bind me to land or times.
I've heaved shovels of humus and hubris over my shoulder,
searching for the golden nugget at the core of my soul.
When I was left with but a six foot hole,
I realized I'd thrown it all away.

Her eyes, too far across the room from me…

Her eyes, too far across the room from me,
are fixed upon the ashen chalkboard words.
Outside the window, whitely-throated birds
are singing in the sun pastorally.
The plush first dandelions of the year,
more yellow than her hair, incense the air.
I picture her and me alighting there,
among the pretty weeds, both leaning near.
But silly scenes like those I see
are still beyond the class's window pane
and called "archaic" and, worse yet, "sweet."
The old professor drones philosophy,
and as our existential hour wanes,
I realize our eyes will never meet.

Their eyes were getting weak, their temples grey…

Their eyes were getting weak, their temples grey--
they passed me going to lunch each day.
A man, a woman, arm in arm
or hand-in-hand with quaint pastoral charm,
warm in the urban cold....

Something like this, in days of old
would merit a poet's style--
a head pillowed on a denim shoulder, a casual smile
softened by words I couldn't write, or hear....
And on into a finite stream of afternoons,
into the maelstrom of shapeless dunes
that mars the passage of time and men,
the couple flowed past my stop and then
into their lives disappeared.

And from an unpastoral future day,
looking back at them and feeling grey,
I realize they don't suffer eternity
that lived their lives happily.

In these, the frenzied frantic e-mail days…

In these, the frenzied frantic e-mail days,
young loves transform their passions into dits
and dahs configured in electric bits
and soundless bytes entangled in the cog-webbed maze.
From somewhere in those dim arrays,
each pulsing pixel like a flint emits
the sparks of souls—true love's prerequisites
come surging through the dark computer ways....
But some romantics of the older styles scoff,
that at a switch's flick, the feelings surge,
the heart strings hum, just fiber optic cable.
And higher bauds make pilgrims easily able
to surrender to the timely loving urge.
But too those switches can quickly be flicked off.

Sometimes on throbbing winter nights…

Sometimes on throbbing winter nights
smelling of uneven engine heat,
my car cuts through the late-gathered rush.
Neon taillights moving crack the starless dark.
Little jigsaw pieces of my life fall from the box.
The future seemed seamless once,
now a shattered mirror mosaic scarred,
what might be broken by what is and what had been.
The jagged little dreams tinkle underfoot
as I march on, lock-stepped with the world.

But then, sometimes on throbbing winter nights
we scatter our tatters on your floor,
mixing metaphors and semantic semaphores, our thoughts,
  our dreams,
incomplete and holy, we can mix their textures together.
From what was and what is,
we'll sew what we've ripped,
making a quilt to wrap ourselves in.

She Sings

She sings notes cut from marble,
Alabama white flecked
with breaths of gold,
edged sharp and clean
into pedestals to lay love lyrics upon.

She sings melodies dressed in cartoon colors,
yellow oranges splashed against a sky,
bearish browns swirling against a thick green,
each primary phrase bleeding distinctly into the next.

She sings textures of thick, rich tresses
curling soft and slow molasses
licked lightly with fire.
The tendrils of song
spilled on a pillow,
smelling of honeysuckle.

She sings, sometimes, to me
still in the night
when the somber silences flutter
down insulating, isolating me
softly in the present.

Lucid Dreaming

Cars are fish outside the windows;
back and forth, again, again.
Darkness steams below;
dusk rolls softly down.
Music burbles through the air
and urban intellect insect noise
behind, around.
Waiting for you, I
breathe warmly, sigh inside.

They say in a dream
you don't know you're in a dream—
but too long I've stretched
for simple moments—
a flashing smile, rolling eyes,
a round hip to lay my hand upon,
the comfortable weight of waiting upon my shoulders—
to miss their concrete flavor....

and with the consciousness,
yesterday's someday is now,
the future oils smeared upon our palette
to dap across the calendars....

The Lady Would Like a Poem

I am not a villain. Hell,
I do my best to perpetrate the art.
I just want my poems to sell.
No way to seduce, but I'm not Astrophel
who taps his words to pour his heart,
but I am not a villain. Hell,
I've versed before and done it well,
but keeping aesthetic value apart,
I just want my poems to sell.
As for love, I'd rather show than tell,
letting deeds, not words impart
I am not a villain. Hell-
bent for prizes, both earthy and angel,
For love or money, I'll do my part.
I just want my poems to sell.
It may well be that the little belle
that rings won't be the cash drawer at the start
I am not a villain; hell,
I just want my poems to sell.

And words are only verbal pantomime,
sweeping gestures made in simple phrases.
I could never prove my love in rhyme,
entangling feelings in semantic mazes.
Sweeping gestures made in simple phrases
satires from the motions of love make.
Entangling feelings in semantic mazes
can strain the heartstrings until they break.
Satires from the motions of love make
some lovers disbelieve the poet's intent, for that
can strain the heartstrings until they break,
making sharply felt chords fall flat.
Some lovers disbelieve the poet's intent, for that
I could never prove my love in rhyme,
making sharply felt chords fall flat.
And words are only verbal pantomime.

No simple sonnet, written with a failing pen,
words scrawled in slants across a legal pad
with scratch-outs black against the printed love
and wrangled words to force a rhyme, like "dove",
could realize the love we have, or had,
before the snapshot words made now a then.
My missing pain is deeper than five feet—
the silly-sweet no realer when expressed.
For you, my heart out-thuds iambic beat;
My heart repeats a spondee in my chest.
Some fourteen lines I've used, at times, to meet
the girls; it's time to give those lines a rest.
When all the couplets end and stop complete,
our love goes on, concrete. I've done my best.

Only when given free, versus poetic constraint,
does love full flower in the day.
for picking seeds and plying manure
and weeding and pruning
and getting and spending
and writing and mowing and trying and trying
can only do so much.
For when love bursts forth,
a splash of color against the world,
the grace is yet divine.

(Like the dove's high coo,
my words, regal wrote, softly spoke—
I hope—soothed her too.)

The temples shook, and low clouds rumbled…

The temples shook, and low clouds rumbled
but somehow I hoped the storm would pass
when the last of my ideals crumbled.
The day was mostly sunny when the Romans tumbled
the walls of Carthage to the salted soil as
the temples shook, and low clouds rumbled.
Like a mailed knight whose steed has stumbled,
I find myself enarmored and on my ass
with the last of my ideals crumbled.
I am the last Romantic shepherd humbled,
alone upon the fields of scorched-earth grass,
these temples shaken before the low clouds rumbled.
All my mantras like myth and magick mumbled,
I flailed and pirouetted an impotent grey mass
to find the last of my ideals crumbled.
I held, white knuckle tight, but then I fumbled
my faith, my fate; I hope the storm will pass.
My temples throbbed, and my low brows rumbled
the day the last of my ideals crumbled.

But through the fifth floor hospital panes…

But through the fifth floor hospital panes
autumn steals slowly in.
The trees, agonizingly clear through ammonia glass, burst
into red gold pyres
for summer to lay its sunsets on.
Slanted roofs slide like days to the next.
Church spires stab the gelling gloom
and clutch the last tracings of light.
They were things once—
now textures, colors and strokes flat behind the glass.
The world blurs Impressionist
as waters trickle down,
and beneath the varnish of medication,
the November son slides into darkness.

I want to hide behind the curtain of…

I want to hide behind the curtain of
your hair, a waterfall that muffles sound
and trickles, falling feathers on, around
my ears, my cheeks, my chin, as we make love.
I want to see your eyes from inches, flush
on furied brow, feel your lips on mine,
your kisses pressing hard until you find
your full, contented smile. Soft fingers brush
that hair behind your ear; I pull it back.
Beyond your hair, outside our secluded sight,
the frozen world grinds fresh white snow to black.
But here, within the artificial night
of scented shadow, snug, our cul-de-sac,
is safe from neon life and modern light.

What End My Words

What end my words that trip across my tongue,
the stressed conceits conceived with skittish pen?
The scattered lines (I hope) are golden when
I toss them lightly, aural candy among
the lately neon caffeinated young.
I seek that one dark corner denizen
whose eyes blink brilliant in the gloom—but then
my flighty moment passes and I'm gone.
My echoes fade into the background night.
My scrambled passions slide from Teflon hearts,
more lowing from the thundering poet herds.
Until my moody movements wrote are right,
until my own life living imitates my arts,
till that elusive day—no end my words.

A Dark Café, Monday, 8:50pm

Shards of souls shattered
scattered on the flagstone floor.
Shredded stream of dreams that mattered
patter lightly on the door
Passed possibilities reflected, refracted,
retracted behind the bottles on the bar.
The shadow's face, his grimace compacted,
impacted by doubts, his love at war.
Awaiting something besides the barkeep's glance,
a chance, perhaps, with someone new about.
But Fate never heralds her advance
and Destiny did not walk in before I walked out.

Consummata

Surrendering to our special silence
we lie a shallow gasp apart,
the rhythm or our breath unbroken in the dusty night.
Trickling fingers down your arm, across your hip,
tracing the contours of smooth muscle beneath velvet skin
as if lightly sculpting the ether of my dreams.
Your belly flickers under fingertips,
I lightly scratch a circle around your heart,
moisten a finger, and mark it with my X.
You do not blink—I do not hesitate—
our self-consciousness melts like chocolate between us
and we drink.

Cliché

Putting my best foot forward, taking two steps back.
Everybody knows bad Men wear black.
Going in circles on the straight and narrow,
breaking my back to suck life's marrow.
Writing between the lines,
every good boy does find
some things are better left to the prose.
My love would be like a well-read rose.
She'd walk in Beauty, clad in starry skies—
but I'd be just like the other guys,
hiding my head in my Shelley, getting my Wordsworth,
chirping like a pair of Keats, for what it's worth.
Bah—it's all been said in Donne,
over and over, again, by everyone.
Just got to take the first step, but it's a doozy.
Since beggars can't afford to be choosy,
I'll settle for a handful of friends.
All's well that, well, ends.

Almost

Almost as dark as the night, her eyes
swept across the buzz of coffee
house chatter and house blenders and lit
once or twice on careless eyes in the corner.
Almost as warm as dark roast, her hair
fell softly to her shoulders like crested
dreams, ebbing into the smoky air.
Almost as smooth as white sand through fingers, my words
unspoken, moments unmade, as time slinks
stealthily to the end of night alone.

Meet My Eyes

Meet my eyes
across the flickering glances of the crowded cafe,
eyes licking lightly across each Other
hoping to catch, hoping to start...
but sputtering, stuttering,
and smoking up our sight.

Hold my gaze
level and even as the Kansas plain
awash with the promise of golden harvest.
The sun beats down, the storms pass over,
but flawless fair-weather eyes come back.

Come to me
through the haze of tomorrow's sepia memories
that drift, stale already, under low lights.
I will tangle you in sticky strands of conversations,
enwrapping you in a tangled skein of possibilities.
We can put our backs to the past,
stare out into the bustling, hustling present,
and realize, yes, this is all that there is,
but not all that has to be.

A slow and sacred dance, between the white…

A slow and sacred dance, between the white
of linen veils and skin, softer, silky smooth,
low syllables intoned and murmured to soothe
the sharp-edged doubts and fears in jagged light
of stark unfiltered moon that pierces night.
Small circles kissed upon the neck, below
the chin, to ripened lips, and cheeks that glow
with vestal fever burning hot and bright.
The candles flicker shadows in your eyes.
We taste the air and each other in scents
of votives, our brushing lips make sacraments.
We weave together fingers, motions, sighs.
When we lie still to cherish our delight
I'll whisper, reminding you our love is rite.

Stopping of a Poem by a Thought

I am not awed by Robert Frost.
I read his poems and I get lost.
Morals are hidden deep inside,
I'll understand at any cost.

The morals he works hard to hide.
Perhaps I'm jealous, I confide.
Yes he can foot and he can rhyme,
and I can't -- believe me, I've tried.

He was a master of his time,
yet some would pay not one lone dime
for Bob Frost's works -- such men are cheap;
they commit literary crime.

His works that do not make me sleep
may cause me to laugh or to weep.
And to some I mutter, "Whoa. Deep."
And to some I mutter, "Whoa. Deep."

Some men will talk about how far they'd go…

Some men will talk about how far they'd go
to win your love, a sacred struggled goal
Some men would trek through harsh Antarctic snow
to plant your flag upon the Southern Pole.
They'd swim the ocean wide to win your love,
dog paddling cross the sea without a break.
They'd climb up to the twinkling stars above,
to prove their tough enough for Heaven's sake.
They'd cross a jungle or desert sands
or run a marathon of miles untold
and crawl to pseudo-Meccas on their knees and hands.
I'm not that wordy and I'm not that bold;
I won't tell you of battles won and lost,
nor of the distance I've already crossed.

A Carved Tree (I)

One day I carved her name into a tree
with mine inside a Cupid-arrowed heart.
When I had closed my knife, she checked my art,
and shook her head, and then she looked at me.
"Now why'd you come and maim this oak?" asked she.
"Here in the woods, it lived its life apart,
but now the awful manly meddlings start.
This tree will never have its privacy."
"I maimed this oak so everyone could see
our names as linked for all Eternity,
and I must admit to you, my deified,
I like our love like this, objectified,
so that it's not another petty 'love',
but like a natural law passed from above."

A Carved Tree (II)

This quiet spot, beneath this ancient oak,
is where I come to think on brooding days.
The open sky is blue and mocks the strays
that cower underneath the leafy cloak.
I sit and sip my slowly warming Coke,
and stumble through my memory, a maze
of many cul-de-sacs of yesterdays.
I remember how, beneath this tree, we spoke....
Above my head, carved by my careful hand,
the heart and letters of a "Brian and ...."
I remember once, the reckless words I said,
in love's embrace of sweetly muddled head.
With human eyes, a truth is now revealed:
That higher laws can also be repealed.

One day, I sprayed her name upon the wall…

One day I sprayed her name upon the wall,
but then it got erased by blasting sand.
I tried again with neon pink in hand,
but later on they greyed my urban scrawl.
"You dope," said she, "what are you trying to do?
Each time you paint my name, they'll cover it,
and take away whatever little wit
you crafted there; your scratching won't show through."
"So what?" I said. "When I've used up my paint,
and both our names inside their little hearts
are blasted by the city's cleansing men,
I'll take some pride in knowing that the taint
of darker paints or sand-scorched building parts
are secret signs of joys that once had been."

Okauchee Light

Across the dark Okauchee lake, a light,
the marker for the end of someone's dock,
is strangely lit at nearly twelve o'clock
and breaks the solid black that is the night.
From here, across the chilling April lake,
through busy bar room glass I see that glow,
but life or rooms beyond I'll never know.
One light does not a utopia make.
Quite like your smile, that single man-made star:
Up there, on stage, you flash a smile at me,
and crinkle eyes to give the gesture weight,
but like the dock-end light, you are too far;
your glow is there for someone else to see,
and now, for me at least, it is too late.

Visions and Revisions: A Prelude for Amy

She sat alone at a table sized for two,
looking bored with nothing to do.
A stack of books, all closed, under her palm;
my breath got thick, but I remained calm.
I just had to get the intro out of my way,
and since it was a coffeehouse, I could easily say:

"Of mocha hair and smoky eyes,
you wire my words and make my soul sweat.
You warm my mind with a steamy mist
whenever I dream of your cinnamon kiss.
Your voice, robust and smooth like Irish creme,
your words are bittersweet, though sharp they seem.
But I see through your metal sheen
to the things you hide and leave unseen
because, my dear, my X-ray eyes
don't stop at your breasts
and don't stop at your thighs.
I see your blood, your bones, your hidden heart,
I hear your fears and I taste your art.
So here I stand, here in the cold,
rapping softly on the door of your soul,
asking to come in and play…."

but I guess that's what they all say.

Perhaps what's needed is for me to say
something special and sweet in a Frenchly way.

"Je t'aime, mon cherie.
Je t'adore, mon ami.
Chercher t'affection."

But I'd hate to give the misconception
that I was just smooth,
and I'd hate to appear to be insincere.

How about a sonnet then, the traditional way
if you've got something in mind that's lovely to say.

"The dryads dance inside their forest glade
and naiads swim among their mirrored pools.
As sirens sing their lullabyes to fools,
Erato verses in her wooden shade.
Athena walks upon Olympus high
and Venus hangs in Italy somewhere.
Young Brigit is hunting down the Celtic hare
and angels live someplace beyond the sky.
So let immortal dreams be dreamt away
in places far removed from you and me,
for I am in this coffeehouse here,
and you, across the table and quite near,
are better than a goddess could e'er be;
for you are real, alive, and of today."

It's a sonnet; not a good one though.
And she deserves the best, better than this I know.
And it's not just that she's there,
it's that she's, beyond compare
that drew me like a moth to a light
in the deep dark of my night.
Whatever I'm to do, I'd best get done
'cause battles not fought are battles not won.
Without a further thought, I walk up and say,
"Good evening, I'm Noggle, Brian J."

And though my words may not have won her heart,
what the hell, it's a start.

Awakening

The sudden lurch and sway of Amtrak steel
awakened me outside of Bloomington.
Grey train-borne snow was blown like things we'd done
beyond the dusty windows, ground beneath the wheel.
The coach car brakes began their banshee squeal.
We burst through the clinging fog, like cobwebs spun
by dark, low clouds before the cleaning sun
could polish up the town and make it real.
The memory of Bloomington and those of her
are scenes within a crystal ball, englassed.
I sometimes shake that sleeping little town
to see that snow aswirl in its blur.
And sometimes when alone, I shake the past
to watch old dreams and lovers flutter down.

Would, dear, my love for you a blanket be...

Would, dear, my love for you a blanket be,
to keep you warm and safe in grip of night?
Would, hon, it touch your trembling arms softly,
to show you I am yours and soothe your fright?
Would, sweet, my love serve as a pillow white,
to complement your sleep with comfort'd smile?
Would, love, it coolly kiss your cheek so light,
to sweeten dreams across a many mile?
Or would my love seem warm for but a while,
then stifle you, a woolen summer shell?
And could my love, through time, become a trial,
and smother you and cause your heart's death knell?
For love you I, but I have fear as well,
my love might bring to you not bliss, but hell.

On a Hill One Afternoon

"Oh my," said he, "This hill gives view to all!
Look there, the purple mountains tower high
with promise of ravines and trees so tall
their branches brush the deep blue sky.
And over there the gleaming sea too calls.
Adventures, fish, and pirates so sly
to plunder ships on which their boom low falls,
to live their days as long before they die."

"But when you look afar you fail to see
the grass, so green that we are sitting on,"
after a pause to pluck a bloom, said she,
"Or smell the flowers, hear the birds' sweet song.
You look to what lie 'cross the distances wide
and do not see the beauty that is beside."

When speaking on the phone with you, Melissa…

When speaking on the phone with you, Melissa,
I lie back on my bed and close my eyes
and flow into a slowly rolling peace
that fogs the mind but blues my sullen skies.
Your tremor trickles down across the line
and rolls across my quickened heart
like raindrops thick upon my roof, supine,
and tracing subtle paths of lovely art.
Your giggle, soft and downy sweet to hear,
all curling, pink, and fluffy dryer warm
I rub against my grizzled cheek and ear
and tangle in my playful snuggling form.
Your words become a velvet fuzzy stream;
though waking I descend into a dream.

A brash young man, ideas set…

A brash young man, ideas set,
an older man with whom he met.
The elder sat on rocking chair
coffee and pipe beside him there.
The boy appraises him with a smile.
The boy said this, after a while:

"How can you sit like that tonight?
The sun's just set, the night's alight
with fun that's calling out to me.
There's stuff to do and things to see.
Music, women, and neon light.
The cars to race, the brawls to fight,
parties to crash, and miles to run.
Tell me, is what you do such fun?"

His piece was said, the boy was smug.
The elder smiled and gave a shrug.
Striking a match, his pipe he lit.
He said, after thinking a bit:

"The cars were fast when I was young.
How loud the songs were that we sung.
On Saturday we stayed out late,
not one was I to ponder fate.
The beer was cool, the days were hot.
Some might regret, but I do not.
The girls were sweet, their lips were wine.
I can not count the loves of mine.
And so, young man, I take some rest.
The years that passed were not the best.
My pleasures now they too are sweet.
Glittering stars, the quiet street.
The night's dark silence, deep and long.
My warm, warm cup of coffee strong.
The soft caress of breeze on cheek,
this type pleasure I try to seek."

The silent boy left in a rush.
The man enjoyed the sudden hush.
He had, in fact, planned what to say,
for he himself once felt that way.

Do not compare the sun to she…

Do not compare the sun to she,
although its light is warm and bright.
And so my love is that to me,
but Sol, not she, gives way to night.

Compare her not to flowered blooms,
of colors bright and scents so sweet.
Of these she is, but winter looms,
and they, not she, will soon retreat.

Her smile, as bright as shines the moon;
they are alike in that extent.
So wax and wane each month, Selune;
I know her smile will be constant.

Of all the things that I have known,
she stands above them all, alone.

My Lead Guitar, Awake!

My lead guitar, awake and roar
in scratching sound and buzzing more.
A song, a song, for precious ears
that are marble made, my love ignore
e'en though my heart been hers for years.

Oh, Mister Drummer bang those skins
with skill and pride, the way that wins
the love of one who loves me not,
though I have sung such metal tunes,
and look how far that I have got.

My vocals screaming start and how
can she ignore their power now?
"Oh baby baby baby babe,
is there a chance, oh please, between
oh you and me, oh maybe, mabe."

My lead guitar, a solo please
so she can think about with ease
the words I sang for her alone.
I hope she knows how much I feel,
that being without her here ain't fun.
My lead guitar, arpeggio,
her ears are deaf to me I know.
She hears not what I sing of her.
The love I feel for her is true,
least for another day or two.

Warrior's Prayer

Oh Thanatos
that stalks the night
to hunt all men,
the wrong, the right.

Oh Thanatos,
whose word is done
I pray this night
we walk as one.

A Haiku

Look, an old photo
A couple with a baby…
Me…Oh, no, I'm old.

Unrequited

The original cover for the chapbook *Unrequited* was a pixelated version of a drawing that St. Louis artist Michael Draga did of me one night at the Venice Café.

"You'll look like that in ten years," he said. I'm pleased to say it's taken me a couple more than that.

Fallen

Tainting the air with plush and homey colors,
snapping oranges and hearth-brick reds
and Cheshire smiles in an intimate dark;
Crisping cheeks and warmly chilling skin
with hearty flush in the windy grey;
Swishing through the thick carpet
of lost summer havens and relief;
Tasting minty decay in the October air;
and sighing soundlessly in the morning night,
I click along and watch my shadow
wax and wane like simple hopes.

A Story

A Prelude (I)

O air, o sweetest air, why flee you so?
My tightened lungs can scarcely keep with you!
A thief, she steals my breath and doesn't know,
this goddess sweet and yet a mortal too.
O words, my wondrous words, where are you now?
The longing songs, the wit I hope I own?
What will I say, what voice, what face, and how?
I must, or find myself again alone.
O voice, my treacherous voice, o fail me not!
Command you I to speak a flowered verse,
or make a jest, I could, I ought!
But what were she to laugh or something worse?
Yet I resolve with steeled heart to try,
I open up my mouth but walk on by.

A Prelude (II)

My thundering youthful heart, beat not so hard,
for volume's strength can never measure love.
Your maddening thuds may put her on her guard,
and now she looks this way, o Lord above!
My reddening cheeks, how dare you color so?
The blood is needed somewhere else, I'm sure,
so cheeks to normal hue, for no winds blow,
and any tint is but a sign to her.
My whitened hands, you tremble with no cause.
No beasts with snarling fangs or bloody cries
are here to threaten me, to give me pause:
no thing to fear, except those sapphire eyes.
To rest, I need to shirk or take the task;
that means to flee, or worse, to simply ask.

A Heartening

But am I not a somewhat virtued man?
No god, tis true, but somewhat more than beast.
No Hercules, no Titan but I can,
with passioned might, hold tightly her, at least.
No Apollo I, but Phoebus has his chore.
Around the earth he daily makes his way,
and I, the mortal one, have less but more,
for she would be the center of my day.
No Zeus am I, no thunderbolts or such,
no power or the wish to take a life,
but then, I lust for but one woman's touch,
remaining true to she, my dreamed wife.
No perfect god could I e'er try to be,
perhaps there's good within my modesty.

A Resolution

No god, but something more than beast am I
and virtues must I have to make me so.
Not swine that roots about his muddy sty,
but I exhume my heart that way, I know.
No sloth who loafs about his treetop bed
and never ventures far from places known.
I am a vigored youth with love unfed,
I must then go the way my heart has shown.
No mouse am I who fears to softly tread
on ground too near to any human frame.
I am a man of couraged heart and head,
who'll call, with hopes and fears aside, her name.
And with a braced heart and hopeful eye
and steady voice shall speak to her, and try.

A Proposal

"O sweetest light that ever graced my eyes,
that made complete the painting of my world
as does the sun when warming bluest skies
or oysters when they're found as lightly pearled,
will you consent to let me warm your nights
when you are cold of chill or cold of heart
and let me salve with care your deepest frights
with healing words which are my only art
and sit with me before the snapping flames
throughout the harsh and snowy winter days
with cider and our talk and loving names
to keep the tender fires within ablaze
--oh, I digress, my question is but this:
will you be mine and share in loving bliss?"

A Rejection

"You silly boy, you talk with dumb big words
that make no sense to human ears like mine
and tangle up your sentences like other nerds
who think they're talking smart and looking fine.
Are words like that supposed to win my heart?
An oyster with a pearl? A sunny sky?
How strange you speak of me! It's hardly art.
I think you are a little out there, guy.
And to propose a 'loving bliss' with you,
well, bliss is not the word that comes to mind.
I'd say a dreadful hell, eternal too,
were I to think of it and be unkind.
So boy, you go and build your cloudy castles,
but I don't need those silly poet hassles."

Angel in the Snow (I)

The sudden snow had fallen like the night.
Saint Louis knew the storm was coming there,
but trembled yet when flakes had filled the air
with patterns that made thick the fuzzy light.
In Mokabe's the coffee cleared my sight,
or maybe just lengthened my covert stare.
I watched you, and I admit I laid you bare
(I must admit it was a rare delight).
But hours too quickly pass in blinding snow
and when love-liking strikes and whites the mind.
I should have walked you to your little car
and seen your lashes laced and cheeks aglow
with winter chill; again my heart declined;
One hundred steps, or one, can seem too far.

Angel in the Snow (II)

It snowed again the Sunday of the play,
and Webster Groves was silent as a bed
is when I've pulled the blanket on my head
to hide my dreams from ever-creeping day.
And as we walked along, I couldn't say
how much I longed to warm your cheeks, all red,
with fingers fresh and warm from gloves I'd shed
to merely touch your lacy skin some way.
I meant to brush my fingertips across your face,
behind your ear and down your snow-touched hair,
to draw you close and warm you from my heart....
I feared a warning glance would end my chase,
a sudden turn away would spark despair,
the blinding sun would pull my dream apart.

Angel in the Snow (III)

It was not mist, but only car exhaust
that rose about you when we said goodbye.
But would it seem too much, a silly lie,
to tell you that I feared the lasting cost,
of battles left unfought, of chances lost,
of sparkling nights when every word and sigh
are clearly dissipating in the dark; Too shy!
It's by myself and not the stars that I am crossed!
The car was idling, throbbing like the blood
that rang an echo in my reddened ears.
I kissed your glove, a pseudo-Spenser stud.
It's not enough, I thought, defying fears,
and then, unlike exhaust, a warming mist
rolled softly through my spirit when we kissed.

Deb of the Dark

The black lights made your shorts a neon glow.
Cut off above the middle of your thighs,
pastel and powder blue, unlike your eyes,
the shorts show all and everywhere you go.
They swish and sway and brush between the chairs
as you bring drinks and smile away the pleas.
You shrug off pats with stiff but practiced ease
and never notice now the drunken stares.
Do other people ever see your smile and lust
to hear your whispers wrought across a meal
or see you walking in the sun's soft light
and watch your eyes awake with sudden trust
and float upon the tide of how you feel?
Or do they only see your shorts at night?

I Curse the Falling Snow

I curse the falling snow these winter days
that flow like ice in slowly-choking streams.
My Fate, or maybe just the jet-stream seems
to mock how much I loved the swirling haze.
I used to wander in Byronic ways,
lost in my faint and fuzzy future dreams
of love, romance, all seen amid the steams
of bated breath and windy teary glaze.
On days when snow falls like curtains on
the cold and greyly-cloaked Milwaukee streets,
I walk alone and yet I'm really not alone;
Inside, among my warm abstract retreats,
I cannot hide in vague potentiality,
not when your glowing face is haunting me....

Pride of My Collection

Your memory, clear and crisp in its matte finish,
I'll put into its little box;
Ten by fourteen and lined with royal velvet,
the box will be your dusty shrine.
I'll put your regretful smile away,
nestled among your apologetic syllables,
and seal them in my deepest vault
with my ritual lack of ceremony
and quietly close the door.
But on silent stormy nights
when rain taps like ghosts
upon my window panes
I'll unlock the heavy door
and hold my heartache against the dark
and see how your memory
catches the shadows well.
I'll revel how it warms my clenched hand
and scratches against my grizzled cheek
and maybe sigh again
before I put it away.

Listening to the Night

I woke and listened to the night.
The furnace hummed and clicked
to spread its artificial warmth.
The darkness rang its droning nothing
and pressed upon me like a heavy blanket.
I could not hear your dreaming gasps,
as light and thick as falling snow
nor the silent tears
that softly cooled my pillow.

Chance Encounter

The day was cold and grey, with chilling sleet
that fell in blurring lines across my sight.
My breath seemed thin and somehow incomplete.
I wondered why I was and why I fight
against the Thanatos within each day.
A car drove by and slushed my wandering fears,
by splashing ice against my trenchcoat, grey,
and slowly sliding down like frozen tears.
But bursting through the dark library door,
a coat of green--I blink and squint my eyes.
A sudden smile and breeze of twirling hair,
you wave before you're lost from sight once more.
And in this world of often futile tries,
a hidden glimpse of hope is often there.

Upon a Snowy Pillow…

Upon the snowy pillow next to me,
your soft blue eyes are closed in lightest sleep.
Your breath is soft and regular and deep;
the sheet is moving slow and steadily.
Your golden hair, a halo, so it seems,
a gentle aura slightly shrouding you.
Your hand is open on your pillow, too,
as if you're reaching out to me from dreams.
I want to reach and lightly touch your cheek
and trace the fleeing shadows down your chin
as stealthy greys forewarn of creeping dawn.
I fear you'll wake and see me tender, weak,
revealing things too tightly held within,
or I will wake and find the vision gone.

Third Floor Eyes

With bouncy strides of legs just lightly tanned,
you walk below my watching third floor eyes.
A gentle wind moves silently and dies;
you brush some wayward hair with careless hand.
Your lips, marooned with hasty morning care,
are framing hinted teeth in sudden joy
and move in greeting of some passing boy,
the words sweet notes unheard in summer air.
Your dark sunglasses never flash my way,
and you continue on toward a class,
or maybe to your dorm--I'll never know.
For sixty stairs is much too far away,
so silently I let you swiftly pass,
invisibly about my way I go.

Diane

Across the swirling smokeless barroom haze
of faces, smiles, uncaring eyes, and beer,
the other people dim as you appear,
a burst of clarity in spring-time's cloudy days.
I want to say the room kaleidoscopes
around your dark and dancing eyes of blue,
and that the stagnant air is fresh with hopes
renewed by but a single smile from you.
I want to tell you all these silly things,
but bars are not the place for poet thoughts,
and English geeks like me are all the same.
With addled head that my despairing brings,
I wander through my tangle of "I-oughts,"
and I am lucky just to catch your name.

Falling Snow

To some the falling snow's a pretty sight
to watch from windows lightly touched by frost
in silence with the one you love, the night
with endless hours of love too quickly lost.
To children it's a cause for hopeful joy
of cancelled school and strongholds built of snow
that should repel attacks their friends deploy
with laughing shouts, they're strafed by a snowball's throw.
To lovers it's a curtain soft and white
that hides them from a colder world without
and keeps their words and hopes from being trite,
as might they seem to those outside in doubt.
To me, the falling snow is something plain,
it's nothing special, just the coldest rain.

Shades of Night

So come and dance before my sandy eyes
elusive and illusive shades of night.
Come tantalize my touch and fool my sight
and buzz my mind with soft synaptic lies!
Portray for me my words and her replies
in subtle shadings of the dancing light.
Her eyes are slowly shifting left to right,
each probing glance fulfilled with whispered cries.
I know that she's not here, dear whirling mind,
and that she's four hundred miles away.
I beg of you to spin your sweet deceit:
no matter what bizarre nightmares you find
to torment me or what plush tricks you play,
they'll pass the time until again we meet....

An Evening Walk

I shrug into my well-worn doubts
and my darknesses swirl like coat-tails
about my lengthened strides
as I pull my fears low over my eyes
and slip into the rain.

Deep Blue Shadows

Deep Blue Shadows

Sometimes the brim casts shadows
deep and blue across my eyes
and coffee's scented grey stings my sight.
From darkened corners
I stare into night-lit spaces
and sip bitter warmth alone.
No street-corner coffee slinger
made his mint crème preaching existentialism
in a melancholic lair—
their humours are light
like the sunshine tomorrow
I'll face with squinty glare,
with clenched and sneering teeth—
but tonight
slow eyes, sardonic swallows,
and deep blue shadows.

Somebody Else's Problem

I. Numbers (The Fall)

A hundred pinkened skies begot a billion stars
Three lovers' moons waned silently
A million breaths in the summer air
Too many words to count
Too few to still the quickened hearts
Two hearts that beat as one
One heart that beat for two;
Two words were said
Two eyes were red
Two eyes grew wide
Two feet beat flight
Two eyes grew redder still.

II. Alone

Alone in her room
behind the barricades
of pastel posters
and bouncy Techno beat,
she puts her head between her pillows
and shivers herself to sleep.

Alone on the phone
across the widest sea
with the confidant who might be her friend,
with the man who might be her lover,
with the stranger who might betray her.
Behind the hiss she awaits the words,
the answer, the right thing to do,
but hears only the clicks of passing time
and wonders if he's there and if he ever was,
but then, softly, a breath.

Alone and unknown
on the strange city streets
she's never really seen before
and is not really seeing now.
She immerses herself
in the impressionist blur of strangers
and they eddy and babble around her,
pleasantly chilly.

III. Letters (The Redemption)

Beyond the simple blocky ABCs and AKBs
and past the swirling loops of her name
the cold MD in the odd OR
with disinterest enters her
as she lies back
and thinks NO NO NO
but doesn't resist
and with her silent screams
and his inhuman skill
the deed is done
and she is deemed OK.

Eternal Shower

From somewhere in the inky darkness
The hours explode like raindrops
Upon my windshield and roll up
And beyond the safety of my now
Going far too fast and lost upon a wandering road.

But in a brief interlude
The seconds slow to a pitter
Upon the roof of the screened-in deck.
We bask in the breeze
As infrequent lightning strobes
And catches shadows in their flight.
We dance slowly through the storm
And shampooed hair clings lightly to my cheek,
And we almost ignore the cold weight of wet
Upon our shoulders.

From somewhere in the inky darkness
Possibility rolls away from my searching high beam
Like fog from an asphalt road.
I'm almost home.

Here Lies A Pedestal For You, My Dear…

Here lies a pedestal for you, my dear,
a fine and Doric cut of marble white.
Ascend it if you wish, and well you might,
and I will kneel before it, never fear.
Oh, I'll adorn it with a flowered wreath
and murmur prayers soft to earn your grace.
I'll daily dust your granite-carved face
and burn incense to sweet the air you breathe.
So climb, my love, up to your lofty perch
and let my arms become your sacred church.
I'll be your keeper if you so desire
and guard your temple gates with jealous ire.
That's if you want to strip the Mystery
and turn our love into idolatry.

Homecoming '93: A Collage

High tide at the Kirkwood Station.
The sea of strangers covers the banks,
and I wade ashore with my gear
on my back and in my hand
to enjoy my vacation.
Upon the wooden platform,
dizzily I spin around, lost,
until above the curling hair
and swirling tide of reunions,
I see my mother's artificial smile.
"How was your trip?" she asks,
cutting through the people.
"Just like the rest," I say.

"What do you think?" my friend asks
over that strange silence
of a strange house in the early morning.
It's three o'clock in Missouri,
and the question argued is
whether one single atom of Helium
placed in the core of the sun
would cause the sun to die.
I hardly know right from wrong
or why I am, much less the quantum physics
bantered about this morning
like sports scores among the intelligent.
I shrug and make a comment
I stole from last month's Discover.
It satisfies him, and he turns to the two strangers
and continues with his argument.
The banter fades to a background music,
and from another room,
someone's mother is talking to demons
who are trying to make her sin,
and I seem to be the only one who notices
and thinks it unusual.

The visit to the rich relations,
unannounced on a rainy night.
My feet were much too wet, I felt,
to walk on their pristine white carpet
as I toured the house.
“That’s where Lisa died,” my mother whispered
as she pointed to a closed door,
the tone of her hushed voice
between conspiracy and self-righteousness.
I don’t know what to say.
“So what are you doing after you graduate?”
The vertigo question of many late nights
I field with a practiced hand.
“Grad school, maybe,” I offer.
I threaten to master the fine arts
and as the words are spoken, the idea,
the project becomes their own.
“Let’s call John,” they say,
the chancellor of a local university,
a United States Senator,
“and get you a, what do you call it,
writing fellowship.”
My mind reels as my idea, in their hands,
becomes a blueprint, a flowchart of my life,
inked by others’ pens, but
“He’s retiring, so he doesn’t owe me anything.”
“Maybe he’ll do it just because.”
“That’s okay,” I withdraw,
“It’s a worthless degree anyway.”
“I thought so but I didn’t want to say anything.”
The songs of politics, of deals,
of money, abstinence, and caution.
Be careful of women in bars,
because condoms break and people die.
learn from the mistakes of others,
they say, and I do, but their point is rather moot.
I’m not very lucky with women in bars anyway.
And so the clock on the stove silently flips its numbers,
and as I stumble through my goodbyes,

my aunt presses a check into my hand.
I put it into my pocket,
and me into theirs.

“Just overwhelming,” the Principal said,
rubbing a thick hand across a suddenly sagging neck.
Then he ordered the parade of unknown names,
freshmen now with world-wise eyes
and collegiate real-life dreams,
across the fluorescent dinge
of overdressed rural pride
of the high school cafeteria.
Up to the obsolete mike they went
with springy steps of youth and hope,
of what they’ve done
and what they might now do,
to shake hands and smile
with nervous little suited men with money.
I applauded politely.

“How are you?” she whispered,
soft, like rustling grass on a summer’s day.
“Kevin,” her mother called,
a distant rumble beyond the horizon.
The blue-grey phone throbbed
a heightened tempo
and its winding cord
stretched to infinity
and disappeared over the edge of the bed.
“Oh, okay, I suppose,” I said,
the stock answer
for those who don’t know,
who never did, and never will.

I taste my salty sweat
and feel it fall like tears, in trails,
as it rolls from my brow.
Unrecognizable music mixed,
continuous bass beating

like an artificial heart
that drives the dancers on.
My frantic rhythmic flailing,
alone, for none venture near
in fear of appearing my partner
is punctuated by my trips to the bar,
to drink a Coke, which draws a frown
from underage girls who lust a drink,
and me for the stamp on my hand.
"Tell us some poetry," the nameless girl asks,
and the girls at the table are not impressed,
but they never are.
Again on the top platform,
I bounce like a crazed aerobic instructor,
watch others sway fluidly together,
and know I don't look like that.
I flail on anyway.

Below my feet is a star for T.S. Eliot,
next to the one for Marlin Perkins.
Around me the shops of the Loop,
the bizarre clothiers whose fashion
is protestation against fashion,
the music stores peddling alternative music,
a normative bashing of institutions,
and the people who participate in both.
Denim clad, I look out of place,
an alien in an alien landscape.
I don't grok anything.
Two friends walk ahead,
enmeshed in their conversation.
I decide not to look the tourist
and ignore the paragraph Eliot rates,
and as I catch up,
I notice my friends fit in.

Water tumbles languidly
behind the nearly distant trees.
A summer breeze rustles the leaves,

and distant dogs cant.
I sit on the back steps,
an oasis of concrete
in the lush greenery of the yard.
Birds titter in the trees,
unknown song that I could learn
if I cared to stay and listen longer.
I wondered if I did
as the sun disappeared behind the hill
and the day slowly faded to black.

The dark outside loosely curtains the train windows,
and dim and murky shapes begin to swim
beyond my vision as the train begins to roll.
I press my face to the cool glass;
dreamily, the lights float by,
like fish in a dark aquarium
that never know they're being watched.
The blonde across the aisle
puts out her cigarette,
lays her head upon her jacket,
and softly drifts to sleep.
Her unmoving form is dim in the windows,
like too many memories.
I recline the purple seat,
close my eyes,
and wonder if the trip
could really be called
a homecoming.

Haiku

We

Breathless faces pressed
Red against the cooling glass
Of our memories

Normalcy

A soft surrender
To downy blankets, quiet nights,
And warm obscurity

Westbound 40

Chasing falling suns
Into night, and then another
Promised tomorrow.

Going in Circles

Going in circles
Around and round builds the force
Of a sling stone's path.

For One Particular Reason

It must have been near seven o'clock,
The evening dragging itself toward the night
Like a sea turtle with a bellyful of life
Onto the sand.
Fatigue was rolling down my neck and settling beneath my shoulders.
My blackened fingers goose-stepped
Across another printed day,
And I divided to conquer some useless number.
I ruled alone,
Beneath the silence of eavesdropped conversations
And amid the echoes of weekends past.
It was then, for one particular reason,
That suddenly again I missed you.

At the Grindstone

Scraping my wit against iron routine
With pretentious dreams poring from my brow,
I rub muscles sour from waiting for breaks.
Between my breaths, my gasps for peace,
And my twisting stretches for contented smiles
I tell myself I am building the strength
To stand erect.

Lay Me Not Bare

Lay me not bare upon your table
to cut apart with your razor eye.
For when you peel back my covering pride
and probe my self-crossing wrath,
you may extract my wandering thoughts,
the dark gossamer of my doubts
and place them beneath my knightly form;
you may pick out my sordid ideals, my pounding heart,
and tack them higher above my head;
you might draw out my encysted past,
carefully unwinding its plenty-tentacles from my soul,
and cast it to my left
and lay my nebulous future to the right;
and you can toss my bloody fears,
my twisted family, torn and atrophied,
and then my blooming coupleted hopes
into their neatly ordered row.
When all your work is done
and I am all revealed,
you might be left to find
there's nothing more to me
than what's in every man,
and you might just wonder
why you cared to look.

A Trophy

Upon the mantle of my memory
Above my roaring soul,
A snapshot image lingers—
Highway headlights strobed
And caught her eyes half crinkled,
A chuckle in her breath—
I'd savored the moment
And swirled her voice in my ears
And still I sometimes do....

Distance salts the garden
And silence shimmers like a veil
Over the delicate petals unfolding
To catch the killer rays of the sun
And as the drought dusts down
And other things to do sprout up,
The futile buds wither in the gloom.

And beneath the fading photo
The green wood stifles the flames
And though it sputters, snaps, and struggles,
My soul seems just to smoke.

Repose

The city grinds on
In the night, when I pause to take a break
And gulp the draught of life
With tightly chested gasps of swallowed air;
The streetlights wink, merry eyes
With knowing nods for weary soles
That wander loosely in the dark….
But cars shush on with destinies
And buzz onto their vanishing points.
The wind like a lover licks
My frantic fevered brow
And murmurs "It's time to go."
The city grinds on in the night,
And so must I.

To Heather, From Across The Years

The sun clung tightly to the river's rocks
as Roddy romped across
pursuing hidden scents and canine games.
The limestone blocks (too hard to lie upon)
were blinding white that burned my eyes.
The comforting darkness of your eyes
and hair fluffing in Spring's last breath
cracked my mouth and enflamed my ears.
Bluebirds and cardinals hummed
somewhere among the bursting trees
and water tickled slowly by.
You moistened playful pouting lips
and murmured slowly
"We're not children now.
I'm a woman; show me you're a man,"
and stepped outside the circle of the day.
"Count my teeth," I said.

An Evening Walk

I shrug into my well-worn doubts
and my darknesses swirl like coat-tails
about my lengthened strides
as I pull my fears low over my eyes
and slip into the rain.

www.ingramcontent.com/pod-product-compliance
Lightning Source LLC
Chambersburg PA
CBHW071639050426
42443CB00026B/768

* 9 7 8 0 9 8 3 2 1 2 3 4 8 *